Vegetarian Cookbook for Beginners

(revised and supplemented)

Over 110 Easy and Healthy Recipes to Get Started

By Maya Perry

Disclaimer and Terms of Use:

Effort has been made to ensure that the information in this book is accurate and complete, however, the author and the publisher do not warrant the accuracy of the information, text and graphics contained within the book due to the rapidly changing nature of science, research, known and unknown facts and internet. The Author and the publisher do not hold any responsibility for errors, omissions or contrary interpretation of the subject matter herein.

This book is presented solely for motivational and informational purposes only.

Table of contents

Introduction

Whether you've choose to go meat-free for moral reasons, practical reasons, or simply because you want to eat healthier, the nutritious recipes in this book can help you to enjoy a vegetarian lifestyle with ease. These delicious meals have been hand-selected to give you the optimal balance of taste, nutrition, and ease of preparation.

The new edition of this book, revised and supplemented, includes more than 110 recipes, including ketogenic ones.

Before you begin looking through the different sections of this book, you may find it helpful to consider some of the following questions:

Why vegetarian?

When done right, a vegetarian diet has a host of benefits, including:

- *Good for our bodies.* Vegetarian diets tend to be rich in fiber and offer good support for nutrients such as folic acids, healthy fats, magnesium, phytochemicals, and many vitamins. Vegetarian diets also have the power to lower your risk of obesity, cancer, and diabetes, and may even improve mood and cognition.
- *Good for the environment.* Growing food, whether we're talking about animal or plant sources, has an environmental impact in greenhouse gas emissions and cost in resources. While not every vegetable on the market has a smaller impact than animal farming, many do. A thoughtfully chosen vegetarian diet can reduce our personal footprint.
- *Respects life.* Vegetarian diets allow us to eat healthy, fulfilling foods that don't require the death of other living animals.

I'm Vegan, Can I Still Use This Book?

With a little adaptation, most of the recipes in this book can easily be transformed for a vegan lifestyle. Use the chart below to make substitutions for egg and dairy products.

Egg or Dairy Product	Vegan Substitution
Shredded Cheese	Cashew shredded cheese
Cream Cheese	Vegan cream cheese (usually coconut oil and tapioca starch based)
Mozzarella	Cashew vegan mozzarella
Parmesan	Toasted almond flour with garlic and herbs
Egg, for quiche	Pureed tofu, salt, seasonings, and almond milk
Egg, fried or scrambled	Pan-seared chopped mushrooms with vegan shredded cheese; mashed acorn squash; scrambled tofu

Principles of Vegetarian and Vegan Eating

If you're new to vegetarianism, you may be wondering what it entails. There are several broad distinctions when it comes to eating fewer animal products:

- Vegetarian (or ovo-lacto vegetarian): Does not eat meat, but does eat other non-meat animal products such as dairy and eggs.
- Ovo-Vegetarian: Does not eat meat or dairy, but does eat eggs.
- Lacto-Vegetarian: Does not eat meat or eggs, but does eat dairy.
- Pescetarian: Follows the same principles as vegetarians, however, fish are acceptable on a pescetarian diet; there is some debate as to whether pescetarianism should be considered a form of vegetarianism.
- Vegan: Abstain from all animal products, including meat, eggs, dairy products, and fish, as well as non-food animal products such as leather and ivory.

There are numerous other subcategories for vegetarianism, but chances are good that you fall into one of these branches. The recipes in this book are either well suited to any of these 5 types of vegetarianism or can be adapted to make them suitable (although there are no recipes that contain fish, many pescetarians eat a largely vegetarian diet most of the time).

Tips for Optimal Nutrition

It's important to ensure that you are getting enough nutrition when eating a vegetarian diet. Keep the following 5 tips in mind as you plan your meals:

- *Eat a variety of foods.* Don't get stuck in just a handful of your favorite vegetables to eat and prepare. Instead, get better nutritional coverage by eating a variety of fruits, vegetables, nuts, seeds, legumes, and grains.
- *Get enough protein.* Make sure to know how much protein your body needs for your age, height, weight, and physical activity level. Plan your meals so that you are able to meet your daily protein requirements with protein-rich vegetables, nuts, seeds, legumes, and eggs or dairy if you consume them.
- *Get enough Omega-3s.* Fish oil is one of the most common sources of omega-3s, which can be problematic for vegetarians. Make sure to include healthy oils and foods with this important nutrient in your diet. Good sources of Omega-3s include coconut oil, avocados, and many nuts and seeds.
- *Get enough vitamins.* Don't assume that because you're eating a lot of fruits and vegetables, you must be getting all of the vitamins that you need. Educate yourself on potential tough spots for your particular school of vegetarianism and make sure to include foods in your diet that contain these nutrients in adequate amounts. You may also want to consider taking a quality multivitamin to help keep your bases covered, however, never use supplements as a replacement for food-based nutrition; they're called *supplements* for a reason.
- *Choose your salts.* Not all salts are created equal. You may want to consider using a Himalayan pink salt rather than your standard table salt as this salt has been reported to

contain a number of important minerals. However, more research needs to be done in this area, so think carefully before choosing a salt for regular consumption. Whichever salt you choose, make sure that you are getting enough salt without straying into the realm of too much.

Prep Time

Most of the recipes in this book can be prepared in under 30 minutes. To further reduce prep time, consider planning your meals 5 -7 days in advance. That way, you can prep more time-consuming items in advance and have them ready on the day of the meal that needs them. For example, if you know you will be having a recipe that requires steamed rice on Monday and again on Thursday, you can save time by making enough rice on Monday to cover both recipes. You can also wash and chop many vegetables a couple of days in advance.

Salads:

Avocado & Feta Salad

Preparation time: 20 minutes

Ingredients for 4 portions:
2 avocados, diced
1 small onion, finely sliced
1/3 cup feta cheese, cut into large pieces
3 cherry tomatoes, sliced fresh
1/3 cup parsley, chopped
1/2spinach, chopped
3-4 tbs. extra virgin olive oil
1 lime, juiced
Salt and pepper, to taste

Directions:
Mix all ingredients in a bowl and stir gently, not to mash the avocados and feta cheese pieces. Add some salt and pepper and serve immediately.

Caprese Salad

Preparation time: 20 minutes

Ingredients for 4 portions:
4-5 cups grape or cherry tomatoes
1 lb. fresh imported Italian mozzarella
1 tbsp. balsamic vinegar (or red wine vinegar for a milder flavor)
10 - 15 large fresh basil leaves, to taste
4 tbsp. of extra virgin olive oil
Italian sea salt, to taste
Black pepper, to taste, freshly ground

Directions:
• Slice tomatoes into halves.
• Cut mozzarella into ¼ - ½ cubes.
• Toss together the tomatoes, mozzarella, olive oil, and balsamic vinegar.
• Tear the basil into large pieces and toss into the salad.
• Season to taste with sea salt and freshly ground black pepper.
• Serve immediately (can be refrigerated to serve a little bit later, too).
Tip: Serve with fresh, crusty bread

Zucchini & Mozzarella Salad

Preparation time: 20 minutes

Ingredients for 4 portions:
1 zucchini, spiralized
1 yellow summer squash, spiralized
20 cherry/grape tomatoes, halved
4 Oz. fresh mozzarella cheese

Lemon Basil vinaigrette:
2 tbsp. lemon juice
2 tbsp. extra virgin olive oil
2 tbsp. white wine vinegar
10 basil leaves, fresh
Salt and pepper, to taste

Directions:
- Combine 2 tablespoons lemon juice, 2 tablespoons extra virgin olive oil, 2 tablespoons white wine vinegar, 10 fresh basil leaves and salt and pepper to taste in a blender or food processor until smooth.
- Divide the squash evenly among bowls with 5 halved cherry tomatoes and 1 Oz. fresh mozzarella.

Serve each salad with about 2 tablespoons of the lemon basil dressing.

Warm Goat Cheese Salad

Preparation time: 30 minutes
Ingredients for 4 portions:

For cheese cooking:
4 pieces goat cheese, sliced 1 inch wide
1 tbsp. whole flour or almond flour to taste, for breading
1 egg
2 tbsp. extra virgin olive oil
Whole-wheat bread crumbs
Any small seeds to liking

For the vinaigrette dressing:
2 handfuls racket: rucola, lettuce, basil leaves, all fresh
1 handful of fresh salad, tied
½ handful linen, chia and grape seeds
½ handful walnuts, chopped

2 tbsp. lemon juice
2 tbsp. extra virgin olive oil
1 tsp. honey
Salt and pepper, to taste

Directions:
- Use the goat cheese right out of the fridge: dip it in the flour, then lay it into the beaten egg and crumbs. Repeat dipping into the flour, egg and crumbs with the seeds.
- Oil the frying pan and put it over medium heat. When hot, fry the goat cheese pieces not more than 2 minutes each side, until

golden and crusty. Then put the goat cheese into the preheated to 350°F/180°C oven and continue cooking it for 5 minutes.
- Mix the honey, extra virgin olive oil and lemon juice in a salad bowl. Put the greenery into the bowl and mix it with the vinaigrette with some salt and pepper if needed.
- Serve the salad on top of the goat cheese pieces.

Sprouted Grain Salad with Eggs and Olives

Preparation time: 20 minutes
Ingredients for 4 portions:
3 cups grain sprouts
1 cup curd soft cheese, chopped in large pieces
4 eggs, boiled
1 small onion, finely sliced
1 cup brined black olives
2 cups iceberg lettuce, fresh
1 clove garlic
3 tbs. lemon juice
4 tbs. extra virgin olive oil
1 tbs. dijon mustard, for a flavour
Salt and pepper, to taste

Directions:
For grain sprouts:
Healthy sprouted grain is freshly cooked and served immediately.
To prepare the sprouts you'll need to wash the grain thoroughly,
several times, and then place them onto the dish or bowl with water
covering the grain for at least a day to three days maximum.
- Combine the sprouts, iceberg lettuce and onions.
- Add the dressing ingredients with the salad, then add the cheese
  pieces, olives
- Add the eggs last, cut into quarters. Put in a bowl without tossing.
  Serve immediately.
Tip: Vegetable ingredients can be changed as you may like.

Veggie & Quail Eggs Salad

Preparation time: 30 minutes

Ingredients for 4 portions:
1 bell pepper,
1 onion, finely sliced
1 celery stalk, striped
7 Oz. green salad, coarsely chopped
1 cucumber, sliced
1 carrot, sliced
5-7 quail eggs, boiled and cut into halves
4-5 tbsp. extra virgin olive oil
Salt and pepper, to taste

Directions:
Place all vegetable ingredients into the salad bowl and mix with salt and pepper seasoning with the olive oil. Add the quail eggs atop. Serve.

Cashew, Spinach and Feta Salad

Preparation time: 20 minutes

Ingredients for 4 portions:
2 tbsp. feta cheese, sliced
½ cup cashews, fried or smoked
1 handful of spinach, fresh chopped
1 handful of arugula, fresh and chopped
½ lemon, juiced
4-5 tbsp. extra virgin olive oil
Salt and pepper, to taste

Directions:
In a salad bowl, whisk the extra virgin olive oil, lemon juice and salt. Add all the greenery ingredients and toss well. Top with the cashews and feta slices.

Greek Salad

Preparation time: 10 minutes

Ingredients for 4 Servings:
4 large tomatoes, cut into small pieces
4 cucumbers, peeled and cut
4 bell peppers, cut in strips
2 red onions, finely sliced
16-20 canned, pitted black olives
7 ounces of Feta cheese, sliced
1 tsp. of dried Oregano
4 tbsp. of Olive oil
1/2 lemon, juiced
Salt and pepper, to taste

Directions:
Slice tomatoes, cucumbers, bell peppers and onion. Place all the vegetables in a bowl. Whisk together the olive oil, oregano, lemon juice, salt and pepper and add to the bowl. Add feta cheese.

Tip: This salad can be prepared 2 hours ahead.

Summer Mix Salad

Preparation time: 10 minutes

Ingredients for 4 Servings:
6 leaves of Romaine Lettuce, torn
6 cherry tomatoes, halved or quartered
1 carrot, grated
1/2 red onion, chopped
1 seedless cucumber (optional)
1 pack seasoned bread croutons (optional)
handful of toasted almonds/pine nuts/walnuts (any)
dried cranberries for garnish

Dressing:
1 tbsp. distilled vinegar or lime juice
1 tsp. Dijon mustard
1 tbsp. honey
2 tbsp. extra-virgin olive oil
pinch of salt, to taste
1 tsp. black pepper, freshly ground

Directions

Mix all the salad ingredients except nuts and croutons in a large bowl.

Prepare the dressing by first adding Dijon mustard in vinegar juice; whisk well. Add freshly ground black pepper, salt, honey mix well. Whisk vigorously while adding extra-virgin olive oil. Spread over the salad, toss, and cover with plastic wrap; keep refrigerated. When ready to eat, top salad with toasted almonds and croutons.

Tip: For a crunchier salad, wash the greens and use a salad spinner to remove excess water from the leaves. Alternatively, you can dab excess water from the leaves with a kitchen towel.

Salad with Beetroot and Goat Cheese

Preparation time: 15 minutes
Ingredients for 4 Servings:
3 blood oranges
2 medium or 3 small beetroot
3 oz. or half a pack of creamy goat cheese
handful of rocket or watercress
3 tbsp. olive oil
sea salt and black pepper, to taste
squeeze of honey
1 tsp. Dijon mustard
1 sprig of thyme leaves, picked
handful of walnut pieces
Directions:
Preheat your oven to 180°c. Scrub the beetroot, then sprinkle with
sea salt and drizzle with olive oil. Wrap beetroot individually in foil
and pop in the oven for about an hour or until just tender. Remove
and leave to cool. Segment blood oranges over a bowl to catch any
juice, then arrange on a plate with some rocket or watercress. Slice
the roasted beetroot into wedges, slice the goat cheese into rounds
and add to the rest of the salad, along with the walnut pieces. In the
bowl with the leftover orange juice, add the honey, mustard, thyme
leaves and some olive oil along with a twist of black pepper. Stir and
taste; add more honey or mustard to your liking. Pour the dressing
over the salad. Serve immediately with some crusty bread.

Roasted Beetroot and Pumpkin Salad

Preparation time: 15 minutes

Ingredients for 4 Servings:
1 lb. pumpkin, deseeded and chopped into ½-inch cubes
1 lb. fresh beetroot, cut into ½-inch cubes
2 tbsp. olive oil
2 tbsp. fresh Basil leaves, shredded
sea salt and black pepper to taste

Directions:
Preheat oven to 180°C. In a baking dish combine pumpkin, onion, beetroot and olive oil. Add sea salt and pepper to taste. Roast for 60 minutes until pumpkin is golden and starting to caramelize, and beetroot is cooked through.
Top with basil and toss gently.

Beetroot and Lentils Salad

Preparation time: 15 minutes

Ingredients for 4 Servings:

1 bunch beetroot, scrubbed, trimmed and halved if large
4 tbsp. extra virgin olive oil
1 tbsp. cumin seeds
1 tbsp. red wine vinegar
1 clove garlic, crushed
1 tsp. Dijon mustard
1 oz. fresh mint, leaves only, chopped
7 oz. lentils
1 small red onion, finely sliced
2 ripe pears, cored and cubed
4 oz. pack watercress, stalks removed

Directions:

Preheat the oven to 200°C, 400°F. Place the beetroot in a roasting tin. Toss with 1 tbsp. of the oil and the cumin seeds, roast for about 35-45 minutes or until tender. In a large bowl, whisk together the remaining oil, vinegar, garlic, mustard, mint and seasoning. Meanwhile, place the lentils in a pan and cover with cold water. Bring to a boil then reduce heat and simmer for 20 minutes until tender. Drain thoroughly, then add to the dressing and toss together. Remove the beetroot from the oven and cut into bite-size chunks. Add to the lentils, red onion, pears and mixed seeds to the salad and toss to combine. Serve piled onto the watercress.

Lentils, Goat Cheese and Olives Salad

Preparation time: 15 minutes

Ingredients for 4 Servings:
1⅔ cups Puy lentils, rinsed
1 carrot, peeled and diced
1 shallot or small onion, finely chopped
2 sprigs of thyme
1 bay leaf
3/4 cup Kalamata olives, pitted and chopped
3 oz. rindless goat cheese, crumbled
2 tbsp. extra virgin olive oil
salt and black pepper to taste, freshly ground
6 oz. mixed baby salad leaves (optional)

Directions:
Place the lentils, carrot, shallot, thyme, and bay leaf in a saucepan with 5 cups of water. Simmer for 15–20 minutes or until the lentils are tender. Drain the lentils well, transfer to a serving bowl, and remove the thyme and bay leaf. Cool until lukewarm. Add the olives, goat cheese, and olive oil, then stir together. Season with salt and pepper. Serve warm.

Variation: Dressed Lentils. Leftovers are good served as a salad. Splash with balsamic vinegar, add extra olive oil, and sprinkle with lots of chopped parsley. If you wish, add sliced anchovy fillets.

Quinoa Salad

Preparation time: 10 minutes

Ingredients for 4 Servings:

3 cups cooked quinoa
1 1/2 cups cucumber slices
10 oz. cherry or grape tomatoes, halved
1/3 cup parsley, chopped
1/3 cup feta cheese, crumbled

Dressing:
1/4 cup lemon juice
2 cloves garlic, minced
2 tbsp.honey
1 tbsp.pomegranate molasses
1/4 cup olive oil
salt and pepper, to taste

Directions:
Salad: In a large bowl, toss together quinoa, cucumber slices, tomatoes, parsley, and crumbled feta. Add the dressing when ready to serve and toss to combine.
Dressing: Combine lemon juice, garlic, honey, pomegranate molasses, and a pinch of salt and pepper in a small bowl. Whisk in the olive oil until the dressing is combined. Check for seasonings and adjust as desired.

Potato Salad

Preparation time: 15 minutes

Ingredients for 4 Servings:
3/4 lb. fingerling potatoes
1 tbsp. olive oil
1/4 tsp. grated lemon rind
1 tbsp. lemon juice
1 tsp. Dijon
1/4 tsp. pepper
1/3 cup arugula, chopped
2 tbsp. Kalamata olives, sliced
1 tbsp. parsley, chopped
1 tbsp. fresh basil leaves, chopped
1 tbsp. fresh chives, chopped

Directions:
Place a saucepan filled two-thirds with water over high heat. Cut potatoes into 1-inch pieces. Add potatoes to pan; cover and bring to a boil. Reduce heat to medium-high. Cook 15 minutes or until tender. Drain.

Whisk together olive oil, lemon rind, lemon juice, Dijon, and pepper in a bowl. Stir in arugula, Kalamata olives, parsley, basil, and chives. Add drained potatoes; toss gently to coat.

Appetizers:

Avocado Sandwiches with Boiled Eggs

Preparation time: 30 minutes

Ingredients for 4 portions:
4 cocoa bread slices or whole meal bread toasts
1 avocado, finely sliced
4 eggs, boiled and cut into slices
Sunflower or other seeds to liking

Directions:
Put the topping in layers on your toasts.

Tip: Add some cucumber for aromatic freshness. This nutritious appetizer is great for breakfast or lunch.

Egg Muffin Cups

Preparation time: 40 minutes

Ingredients for 4 portions:

4 eggs
1 large onion, chopped
1 red Bell pepper, chopped
1 cucumber, grated
2 handfuls spinach, finely chopped
½ cup parsley, cut small
3 tbsp. extra virgin olive oil
1 tbsp. wheat flour
Salt and pepper, to taste

Directions:
Grease the pan with the olive oil. Simultaneously add onion, pepper and cucumber into the pan and mix it, stir for 3 minutes. Remove from fire and place this vegetable mixture into your silicone cupcake moulds.
Beat the eggs with flour and salt, add the chopped spinach and parsley into the egg mixture. Pour the egg mixture on top of the cupcake moulds and place them into the preheated to 350°F/180°C oven. Bake for 20 minutes.

Serve warm.

Zucchini Wraps

Preparation time: 30 minutes

Ingredients for 4 portions:
2 zucchini, finely sliced lengthwise
1 cup parmesan cheese, cut large
2 tbsp. lemon juice
1 tbsp. extra virgin olive oil
1 pinch of parsley or basil or any fresh herb to taste
Salt and pepper, freshly ground, to taste

Directions:
Make a layer of 3 long zucchini slices each laying on top of each other to form a circle. Place a large piece of parmesan cheese onto the zucchini layer and wrap it. Make 4 portions using all the ingredients.
Sprinkle the zucchini wraps with extra virgin olive oil and lemon juice, place them into the oven at the medium heat and have them baked for 5 minutes.
Serve warm with a pinch of the fresh herbs on top.

Egg Wraps

Preparation time: 40 minutes

Ingredients for 4 portions:

4 eggs
2 tbsp. wheat or banana flour
1 Avocado, sliced
3 small tomatoes, diced
10 Basil leaves, cut
1 handsful parsley, fresh and cut
½ cup almonds and peanuts, chopped
1/3 cup linen seeds for the egg wraps
1 tbsp. Extra Virgin Olive oil
1 pinch of parsley or basil or any fresh herb to taste
Salt and pepper, freshly ground, to taste

Directions:

- You can have them cooked ahead of time and fill them with any ingredients as desired.
- Oil the frying pan with the extra virgin olive oil and heat it over the medium temperature.
- In a bowl, mix eggs well with a whisk adding flour, a pinch of salt and linen seeds.
- Pour the egg mixture into the preheated pan and tilt pan to spread the egg into a large circle, forming a fine egg pancake.
- Let it cook half a minute on each side.
- When removed from pan, have the egg wraps fully cooled.
- Top them with vegetable filling with nuts and greenery, roll and serve warm or cold.

Quiche Lorraine with Spinach

Preparation time: 1 hour 20 minutes

Ingredients for 4 portions:
Dough:
2 and ½ whole wheat flour
½ cup butter
1 tsp. salt
1 tsp. sugar
½ cup vegetable shortening
½ cup water
Filling:
4 eggs
1 and ½ cup of cream
½ package spinach, frozen, well drained / 7 Oz. spinach, fresh and chopped
1 cup swiss cheese, shredded
1 small onion, diced
2 tbsp. nut, ground
2 tbsp. extra virgin olive oil
Salt and pepper, to taste

Although traditional Quiche Lorraine is cooked without spinach, the recipe fully reflects the tradition and is perfect for a brunch!

Directions:
Mix all dry dough ingredients with butter and shortening (e.g. in a food processer). Add water and knead your dough a bit. In a plastic wrap, place it into a fridge for an hour. Roll out the crust and press the dough on the bottom and the sides of the dish to fit the extra

from the sides. In a boiling water have 2 eggs boiled and dice them. Combine the remaining eggs, cream and add salt with pepper. In a frying pan sprinkle some oil, add the onion and stir it for 8-10 minutes until onion is almost transparent. Layer the cheese, the boiled eggs, the eggs mixture, the onion, and the spinach on top of it. Bake it in a preheated to 350°F/180°C oven for 20 minutes until the crust is cooked well. Top with some freshly ground nuts.

Tip: Served best at close to room temperature warm.

Quiche Lorraine with Tomatoes and Mushrooms

Preparation time: 1 hour 20 minutes

Ingredients for 4 portions:

1 whole wheat dough crust, rolled (use the dough recipe as in the above Quiche Lorraine with Spinach)
15 Oz. portobello mushrooms, sliced
1 large onion, chopped or diced
1 cup cheese, shredded
½ cup milk
2 eggs
10 cherry tomatoes, fresh
1 bunch of dill, spring onion and parsley, fresh, chopped into small pieces
2 tbsp. extra virgin olive oil
Salt and pepper, to taste

Directions:

- Oil the baking dish and place the rolled crust onto it, add half of the cheese minced and bake it in an oven for 10 minutes (170 Degrees).
- Mix milk with the eggs and cheese.
- Place mushrooms and onion into the frying pan and cook until onion is transparent.
- Layer the cooked mushrooms onto the crust and salt and pepper to taste, add the fresh greenery and place the tomatoes last.
- Pour the eggs-and-cheese mixture atop.
- Bake until done (at 350°F/180°C) for 30 minutes.

Quiche Lorraine with Seasonal Vegetables

Preparation time: 1 hour 20 minutes

Ingredients for 4 portions:
1 whole wheat dough crust, rolled (use the dough recipe as in the above Quiche Lorraine with Spinach)
1 red bell pepper, cut into large stripes or other
1 yellow pepper, cut into stripes or other
1 red onion, sliced
1 zucchini, diced
4 eggs
4 ½ Oz. fluid cream/milk
4 Oz. Cheddar cheese
1 bunch of spring onion or any seasonal herb, to taste
Salt and pepper, to taste

Directions:
- Roll out the crust and place it into the oiled baking dish so that it covered the sides of it. Bake for 5 minutes in a preheated to 350°F/180°C oven and then return to your cooking table.
- Place all the vegetables onto the baking sheet, sprinkle them with olive oil and bake for 10 minutes then cool them.
- Mix milk with the eggs and cheese, add some salt and pepper to taste and any herbs you like.
- Spread the vegetables onto the crust and pour the eggs mixture on top.
- Bake 30 minutes more until crust is light-brown.

Grilled Vegetable Rolls

Preparation time: 20 minutes
Ingredients for 4 Servings:

Aubergines:
3 medium aubergines
1 tsp. cumin seeds, toasted
1 pinch of salt
4 ½ tbsp. olive oil

Quinoa and paneer filling:
3 ½ oz. quinoa
1 small onion, chopped
1 tsp. ginger-garlic paste
1/4 tsp. ground turmeric
3 ½ oz. paneer, grated
1 tsp. garam masala powder
1/4 bunch coriander, chopped
1 dash vegetable oil
1 tsp. salt

Crunchy vegetables:
1 red beetroot, coarsely grated
2 carrots, coarsely grated
1 red pepper, cut small

Directions:

Aubergines: Rinse the quinoa thoroughly and prepare according to packet instructions, cooking in either stock or water. Once cooked, drain off excess liquid and set aside. Combine 3 ½ tablespoons of olive oil, the toasted cumin, and salt in a bowl, then mix together to make the marinade. Cut the top off of the aubergines before cutting lengthways into 4mm thick slices. Brush the aubergine slices with the marinade. Aubergine are thirsty vegetables - they soak up a lot of oil and dry out and crisp up easily, which in this case we don't want, so brush with more oil if necessary.

Add a tablespoon of olive oil to a large frying pan or griddle pan and set over a medium heat. When the oil is hot, add some of the aubergine slices and fry for 2-3 minutes on each side until they soften and have a nice golden color, then lay them out on some kitchen paper to absorb any excess moisture. Continue to cook in batches until all of the slices are ready.

Paneer and Quinoa Filling: To make the paneer and quinoa filling, add a dash of vegetable oil to a nonstick pan and place over a medium heat. When the oil is hot, add the chopped onion and fry until golden. Stir in the ginger-garlic paste, ground turmeric, salt and chili powder and fry for 2 minutes more. Add the quinoa, cook for 5-7 minutes then sprinkle in the grated paneer. Stir, remove from the heat then sprinkle over the garam masala powder and chopped coriander. To assemble, lay out the grilled aubergine slices on a chopping board. Spread a generous layer of the paneer and quinoa filling on top of each and sprinkle over the beetroot, carrot and red pepper. Wrap each slice around the filling to create a roll. Stack the rolls onto a large plate and serve immediately.

Sweet Potato Starter

Preparation time: 20 minutes

Ingredients for 4 Servings
8 sweet potatoes, well washed and cut in halves or sliced
3 tomatoes, sliced
10 canned, pitted black olives, sliced
1 cup cottage cheese or goat cheese, or any creamy cheese you prefer
1 fresh lime, quartered
3 tbsp. olive oil
1 pinch of parsley or any other herb to your liking, chopped
salt and pepper, to taste

Directions
Brush the baking sheet with oil. Place the cut potatoes on the sheet, sprinkle with olive oil, and add salt and pepper to taste. Bake in an oven for 15 minutes at 180°C or 350°F. Before serving, top the potatoes with cheese, black olives and tomatoes. Sprinkle some lime juice and olive oil. Add dry herbs for garnish and flavor.

Tip: You can use a variety of toppings for potato bites, so don't be afraid to experiment!

Dips:

Pesto Sauce

Preparation time: 40 minutes

Ingredients for 4 portions:
2 cups baby spinach leaves
1 cup basil leaves
5 gloves garlic, cut into large pieces
1/3 cup pine nuts
½ tsp. red pepper, crushed, to taste
1 lemon, juiced
½ cup extra virgin olive oil
Salt and pepper, to taste

Directions:
- Blend all the ingredients with several tablespoons of the extra virgin olive oil in a food-processor until almost smooth. Scrape the sides of the bowl when necessary.
- Sprinkle the extra virgin olive oil into the mixture gradually while processing.
- When smooth, can be served immediately.
Should be kept in a fridge not more than a week.

Avocado Dip

Preparation time: 5 minutes

Ingredients for 4 portions:
2 ripe avocados, pitted
½ can plain Greek yogurt
2 cloves garlic, minced
1 lime, juiced
Kosher salt
Black pepper, freshly ground

Directions:
- Mash avocados in a large bowl.
- Add yogurt, garlic, and lime juice to the bowl.
- Serve seasoned with salt and pepper.

Tzatziki Greek Dip

Preparation time: 20 minutes
Ingredients for 4 portions:
2 medium cloves garlic
1 medium cucumber
1 cup Cabot plain low-fat Greek yogurt or Cabot plain Greek yogurt
1 tbsp. lemon, freshly juiced
1 tbsp. extra virgin olive oil
1 tbsp. fresh dill weed, finely chopped
¼ tsp. salt, plus more to taste
½ tsp. black pepper, freshly ground
Directions:
- Peel garlic and chop coarsely. Sprinkle with ¼ teaspoon salt and mash into puree with blade of knife held sideways. Scrape into medium bowl.
- Remove ends from cucumber and peel. Cut in half lengthwise; scrape out and discard seeds. Coarsely grate cucumber flesh or mince finely with knife.
- Working over another bowl or sink, squeeze grated or chopped cucumber firmly to extract as much juice as possible; discard juice and add squeezed flesh to bowl with garlic.
- Add yogurt, lemon juice, olive oil, dill and pepper, stirring together well.
- Cover and refrigerate for at least 2 hours for flavors to blend.
Serve as dip with pita bread and fresh vegetables.

Classic Hummus

Preparation time: 20 minutes

Ingredients for 4 portions

3 cloves garlic, minced
1 can chickpeas, drained and rinsed
1 tsp. kosher salt
¼ cup tahini
¼ cup lemon juice, to taste
1 tbsp. extra virgin olive oil, more for drizzling on top
Paprika for garnish

Directions

- Add the garlic, chickpeas, kosher salt, tahini, lemon juice and 1 tablespoon of olive oil to your food processor and process until it is well combined and has a thick creamy texture. If it is too thick you can thin with additional lemon juice or additional olive oil.
- Put into a bowl, and with a spoon, make some valleys or rivers in it for some olive oil to get added on top.
- Finally, garnish with paprika if you like.

Beetroot Hummus

Preparation time: 10 minutes

Ingredients for 4 Servings:
1/2 lb. beets (about 4 medium sized beets)
2 tbsp. tahini sesame seed paste
5 tbsp. lemon juice
1 small clove garlic, chopped
1 tbsp. ground cumin
1 tbsp. lemon zest (zest from approx. 2 lemons)
generous pinch of sea salt or Kosher salt
freshly ground pepper, to taste

Directions:
Cook the tops from the beets, scrub the roots clean, and put them in a covered dish with about ¼-inch of water. Place in a 190°C or 375°F oven and cook until easily penetrated with a knife or fork. Alternatively, cover with water in a saucepan and simmer until tender, about 30 minutes. Peel once they have cooled.
Place all ingredients in a food processor (or blender) and pulse until smooth. Taste and adjust seasonings and ingredients as desired. Chill and store in the refrigerator for up to 3 days or freeze for longer storage.
Tip: Eat with pita chips, sliced cucumber or celery, or on a crostini with goat cheese and shaved mint.

Roasted Peppers Dip

Preparation time: 15 minutes

Ingredients for 4 Servings:
2 medium red bell peppers
1 tbsp. garlic, minced
1 tsp. extra-virgin olive oil
1 tbsp. balsamic vinegar
1 cup sour cream
1 tbsp. basil, finely chopped
salt and pepper, freshly ground

Directions:
Roast the peppers over a gas flame or under the broiler until charred all over. Transfer to a bowl, cover with plastic wrap and let steam for 20 minutes. Discard the skins, cores and seeds. Pat the peppers dry and finely chop them. In a skillet, cook the garlic in the oil over moderate heat until fragrant, about 30 seconds. Add the peppers and vinegar and cook over moderately low heat, stirring until dry, about 12 minutes. Transfer to a bowl to cool. Stir in the sour cream and basil and season with salt and pepper. Refrigerate until chilled.

Soups:

Mushrooms Soup

Preparation time: 40 minutes
Ingredients for 4 portions:

1 large white onion, diced
1 package (10 Oz.) white button mushrooms, sliced
1 package (10 Oz.) baby portobello mushrooms, sliced
10 stalks thyme, fresh, leaves removed
½ cup heavy cream (36%-40%)
1 cup organic vegetable broth
1 tbs. tapioca flour
1 cup almond or cashew milk (unsweetened)
1 dried bay leaf
½ tbs. liquid aminos (GF) (or soy sauce)
½ tsp. salt
Pepper, freshly ground

Directions:
- In a large saucepan, over medium heat, add the diced onions. Allow to sweat while slicing the mushrooms. About 5-7 minutes. Move onions to the sides of the saucepan and add mushrooms, allow to cook 5 minutes uncovered. Stir the onions and mushrooms together. Add fresh thyme and allow to continue to

cook, at least 10 minutes. You will notice a substantial amount of water has come out of the mushrooms, and they are reduced in volume by half.

- Add the bay leaf, the salt and the liquid aminos to the mushrooms.
- Stir the 1 tbs. of tapioca starch into the organic broth. Add to mushrooms and stir with the cream. Add almond milk. Allow to cook for at least 15 minutes, stirring occasionally. Taste and add freshly ground black pepper to taste.

This soup is amazing the next day as well and can easily be doubled. Add cashew cheese or enjoy the soup just as it is!

Asparagus Soup

Preparation time: 40 minutes

Ingredients for 4 portions:
2 bunches asparagus (about 2-1/4 pounds)
3 tbsp butter, unsalted
2 medium yellow onions, chopped
3 cloves garlic, peeled and smashed
6 cups vegetable broth
Salt
Black pepper, freshly ground
2 tbsp. lemon juice, freshly squeezed
¼ cup parmigiano-reggiano, grated
Handful herbs, such as thyme, dill or basil (optional, for garnish),
fresh

Directions:
- Melt the butter in a large pot over medium heat.
- Add the onions and garlic and cook until soft and translucent,
  about 10 minutes.
- In the meantime, cut the tips off of the asparagus spears and set
  aside.
- Cut the remaining spears into ½-inch pieces.
- Add the chopped asparagus (except for the tips) to the pot, along
  with the vegetable broth, 1 teaspoon salt and ¼ teaspoon pepper.
- Bring to a boil, then cover and turn heat down to low. Simmer for
  about 30 minutes until vegetables are very tender.

- Meanwhile, bring a small pot of salted water to a boil. Cook the reserved asparagus tips for a few minutes until tender-crisp. Drain and refresh under cold water or in an ice bath. Set aside.
- Purée the soup with an immersion blender until completely smooth. (Alternatively, use a standard blender to purée the soup in batches, then return the soup to the pot.) If necessary, pass the soup through a fine sieve to remove the fibers (the best way is to place the sieve over a large bowl, then use a ladle to push the soup through in circular motions).
- Return the soup to the pot and bring back to a simmer. Stir in the lemon juice and grated parmigiano-reggiano.
- Taste and adjust seasoning with salt, pepper and more lemon juice if desired (you may need up to a teaspoon more salt).

Ladle the soup into bowls, then top each bowl with asparagus tips, fresh chopped herbs, more grated parmigiano-reggiano and freshly ground black pepper if desired.

Creamy Spinach Soup

Preparation time: 40 minutes

Ingredients for 4 portions:
2 tbsp extra virgin olive oil
2 eggs, boiled and cut in half
10 Oz. spinach, fresh
2 cloves garlic, finely minced
½ medium onion, chopped
4 tbsp. (½ stick) butter
¼ cup almond wheat flour
3 cups whole milk
2 tsp. kosher salt, or more to taste
½ tsp. cayenne pepper, or more to taste

Directions:
- In a large skillet, heat the olive oil over medium heat.
- Add the spinach and garlic and cook, stirring constantly, until the spinach is wilted, 2 to 3 minutes.
- Add the mixture to a blender or food processor, pour in ¼ cup hot water and pulse until pureed. Set aside.
- In a large soup pot, cook the onions in the butter over medium heat until the onions begin to soften. Sprinkle the flour over the top and stir to combine. Cook for about 2 minutes, then pour in the milk, stirring occasionally.
- Add the salt, cayenne and some black pepper and stir to combine. Cook over medium heat for 5 minutes, stirring constantly.

- Pour in the pureed spinach, then cook until thickened, another 3 to 5 minutes.
- Check the seasonings, adding more salt, black pepper or cayenne as needed.

Serve warm and immediately.

Broccoli Cheese Soup

Preparation time: 40 minutes

Ingredients for 4 portions:
16 Oz. bag broccoli florets
8 Oz. cheddar cheese, shredded
3 eggs, boiled, cut in cubes
4 tbsp. butter
1 onion, chopped
3 carrots, sliced in rounds
2 cloves garlic, finely chopped or grated
¼ cups whole wheat flour
2 cups milk
2 cups vegetable broth
1 bay leaf
Salt and pepper, to taste

Directions:
- Splash the butter to the saucepan or soup pot.
- Add onion, carrots, garlic and cook for 5 minutes.
- Add the remaining butter and whisk in the flour gradually until combined.
- Add the milk and whisk on until combined.
- Pour the vegetable broth and bring it to the boil.
- Add the broccoli florets, seasoning salt and pepper and cook for 20 minutes more.
- Place the boiled ingredients into the food processor and mix until pureed.

- Pour the puree into the saucepan again and add the cheese, bay leaf and stir melted until combined for several minutes more.

Remove from heat, remove the bay leaf, cool and serve it seasoned with salt and pepper to your liking.

Creamy Leek Avocado Soup

Preparation time: 40 minutes

Ingredients for 4 portions:
1 avocado, skin removed
2 leeks, cut into rings
15 Oz. canned white beans, drained
1 onion, chopped
2 cups vegetable broth
1 tbsp. extra virgin olive oil
1 clove garlic, sliced
Dill and green onion for serving
Salt and pepper, freshly ground

Directions:
- In a large pan pour the tablespoon of extra virgin olive oil over the medium heat, add the leeks and stir-fry for several minutes until golden brown.
- Remove part of the leeks and set aside.
- Add onion and garlic and cook until soft and transparent.
- Pour the vegetable broth into the saucepan and add the beans and simmer for 15 minutes covered.
- Cool before you place it into the blender.
- Add the avocado and salt and pepper and blend it until well combined. Add some broth if it is too thick.

Serve topped with fresh herbs, leeks you've removed earlier and onions

Coconut Curry Pumpkin Soup

Preparation time:40 minutes

Ingredients for 4 portions:

1 onion, chopped coarsely
1 small pumpkin, chopped into cubes, seeds removed
2 tomatoes, chopped
3 tsp. curry powder
6-7 Oz. coconut cream / not full fat coconut milk
¾ cup heavy cream
3 cups vegetable broth
2 tsp. ginger, grated
Salt and cayenne pepper to taste

Directions:

- In a large pot add onion and cook it without the lid until light brown.
- Add the pumpkin cubes, curry powder and seasoning spices.
- Sauté for several minutes and add the vegetable broth and bring to the boil.
- Cover the pan and simmer for about 30 minutes over low heat.
- Add coconut cream and milk cream.
- Place all the ingredients in a blender and mix until creamy.

Serve with the pumpkin seeds and cream.

Tomato Soup

Preparation time: 15 minutes

Ingredients for 4 Servings:
For the soup:
1 tbsp. olive oil
1 tbsp. butter, unsalted
1 medium yellow onion, medium diced
kosher salt
2 medium garlic cloves, minced
pinch of red pepper flakes (optional)
1 (28 oz.) can whole peeled tomatoes, preferably San Marzanos
1½ cups of water
1/3 cup heavy cream
freshly ground black pepper, to taste

Optional garnishes (alone or in combination):
extra-virgin olive oil
4 fresh basil leaves, julienned
parmesan cheese, freshly grated

Directions:
Place a medium saucepan over medium-low heat and add the oil and butter. When the butter melts, add the onion and a big pinch of salt. Cook, stirring occasionally, until the onion is completely soft,

about 15 minutes. If at any point the onion looks like it's beginning to brown, reduce the heat. Add the garlic and optional red pepper flakes and cook for 5 minutes more, stirring occasionally.

Increase the heat to medium and add the tomatoes and their juices to the pan. Roughly crush the tomatoes with the back of a wooden spoon and cook until they're hot and beginning to soften, about 10 minutes. Add the broth or water and bring to a simmer. Cook at a medium simmer until the tomatoes begin to fall apart, about 15 minutes.

Remove the soup from the heat and cool slightly, about 10 minutes. Purée the soup directly in the saucepan using an immersion blender, or use a countertop blender, carefully puréeing the soup in a couple of batches until smooth.

Return the soup to the burner over low heat and stir in the cream. Add black pepper, then taste and adjust the seasoning with additional salt or pepper as needed. Serve in warmed bowls as is or topped with the garnishes of your choice.

Lentil & Tomato soup

Preparation time: 20 minutes

Ingredients for 4 Servings:
1 tbsp. olive or vegetable oil
1 large onion, finely chopped (1 cup)
1 medium stalk celery, cut into ½-inch pieces
2 cloves garlic, finely chopped
2 medium carrots, cut into ½-inch pieces (1 cup)
1 cup (8 oz.) lentils dried sorted, rinsed
4 cups water
4 tsp. vegetable bouillon granules
1 tsp. thyme leaves, dried
1/4 tsp. pepper
1 bay leaf, dried
1 can (28 oz.) organic diced tomatoes, undrained

Directions:
Heat oil in a 3-quart saucepan, over medium-high heat. Add onion, celery and garlic; cook about 5 minutes, stirring occasionally, until softened. Stir in remaining ingredients except tomatoes. Heat to boiling. Reduce heat; cover and simmer 15 to 20 minutes or until lentils and vegetables are tender. Stir in tomatoes. Reduce heat; simmer uncovered about 15 minutes or until thoroughly heated. Remove bay leaf.

Pumpkin Soup

Preparation time: 5 minutes

Ingredients for 4 Servings:
2 lb. pumpkin (any), chopped into large chunks (remove skin and seeds)
2 medium onions, sliced
2 cloves of garlic
3 cups of vegetable stock
1 cup milk
salt and pepper

Directions:
Combine all ingredients (except salt and pepper) in a saucepan and bring to boil, then reduce heat and let simmer until pumpkin is tender. Remove from heat and use a stick blender to blend until smooth. If you don't have a stick blender, use a blender.
Season to taste with salt and pepper, then serve with crusty bread.

Variations: For a richer finish, substitute the milk with cream, but add after blending and do not bring to boil.

Garnishes: Dollop of yoghurt, sour cream or creme fraiche goes wonderfully.

Minestrone Soup

Preparation time: 25 minutes

Ingredients for 4 Servings:

1 tbsp. olive oil
1 medium brown onion, finely chopped
1 celery stalk, trimmed, finely chopped
1 large carrot, peeled, chopped
2 garlic cloves, crushed
4 cups Massel vegetable liquid stock
2 tbsp. tomato paste
3 large ripe tomatoes, chopped
3/4 cup Vetta small shell dried pasta
12 oz. can cannellini beans, drained, rinsed
2 small zucchinis, chopped
1/2 cup peas, frozen
1/2 cup roughly chopped fresh basil leaves
parmesan cheese, finely grated, to serve

Directions:

Heat oil in a large saucepan over high heat. Add onion, celery, carrot and garlic. Cook, stirring, for 3 to 4 minutes or until onion has softened. Add stock, tomato paste, tomato and 1 cup cold water. Bring to the boil. Reduce heat to low. Simmer for 30 minutes or until vegetables are tender. Add pasta, beans, zucchini and peas. Simmer until pasta is tender. Stir in basil. Top with cheese.

Hot dishes:

Veggie Balls

Preparation time: 40 minutes

Ingredients for 4 portions:

1 large onion, finely chopped
½ cup sunflower or rapeseed oil for frying
1 red bell pepper, finely chopped
 2 carrots, finely chopped
2-3 cloves garlic, minced
1 cup kale, chopped or minced
12 Oz. cauliflower, minced
2 tbsp. extra virgin olive oil
1 tbsp. vegetable stock powder
½ cup almond or whole-wheat flour
Flour mixed with linen and sesame seeds for dusting
Salt and pepper, to taste

Directions:
- Boil the cauliflower for 5 minutes and then drain. In a food-processor blend it with the extra virgin olive oil until smooth.
- Cook the onion with garlic in a preheated saucepan over medium heat for a minute.
- Add carrots to onion, pepper, cooked peas and kale. Let it cook over a medium heat.

- Add some stock powder, gram flour and season thoroughly with salt and pepper. Mix all the ingredients and remove from heat.
- Sprinkle your hands and chopping board with a little flour mixed with linen and sesame seeds.
- Roll the teaspoon-size mixture into the balls and place them onto the board. You might have about 20 vegetarian "meatballs".
- Pour some oil into the frying pan with seed or sunflower oil, and fry the meatballs, turning them until they are golden-brown all over. Remove from the frying pan to a plate with a kitchen towel/paper to drain the extra virgin olive oil.

Serve the meatballs with the sauce you prefer poured over the top, with any hot dish you prefer.

Grilled Vegetable Rolls

Preparation time: 20 minutes

Ingredients for 4 portions:
For the aubergines:
3 medium aubergines
1 tsp. cumin seeds, toasted
1 pinch of salt
4 ½ tbsp. extra virgin olive oil
For the quinoa and paneer filling:
3½ Oz. feta cheese, grated
3 ½ Oz. paneer, grated
1 small onion, chopped
1 tsp. ginger-garlic paste
¼ tsp. turmeric, ground
1 tsp. garam masala powder
¼ bunch coriander, chopped
1 dash vegetable oil
1 tsp. salt
1 pinch sesame seeds
For the crunchy vegetables:
1 red beetroot, coarsely grated
2 carrots, coarsely grated
1 red pepper, cut small

Directions:

- Combine 3 ½ tablespoons of extra virgin olive oil, the toasted cumin and salt in a bowl, then mix together to make the marinade.
- Cut the top off of the aubergines before cutting lengthways into 4mm thick slices. Brush the aubergine slices with the marinade. Aubergine are thirsty vegetables - they soak up a lot of oil and dry out and crisp up easily, which in this case we don't want, so brush with more oil if necessary.
- Add a tablespoon of extra virgin olive oil to a large frying pan or griddle pan and set over a medium heat. When the oil is hot, add some of the aubergine slices and fry for 2-3 minutes on each side until they soften and have a nice golden colour, then lay them out on some kitchen paper to absorb any excess moisture. Continue to cook in batches until all of the slices are ready.
- To make the paneer and feta cheese filling, add a dash of vegetable oil to a nonstick pan and place over medium heat. When the oil is hot, add the chopped onion and fry until golden.
- Stir in the ginger-garlic paste, ground turmeric andsalt and fry for 2 minutes more.
- Add the feta cheese, cook for 5-7 minutes then sprinkle in the grated paneer. Stir, remove from the heat then sprinkle over the garam masala powder and chopped coriander.
- To assemble, lay out the grilled aubergine slices on a chopping board. Spread a generous layer of the paneer and Feta cheese filling on top of each and sprinkle over the beetroot, carrot and red pepper. Wrap each slice around the filling to create a roll.

Stack the rolls onto a large plate and serve immediately.

Baked Eggplant with Cheese

Preparation time: 30 minutes

Ingredients for 4 portions:
3 tbsp. extra virgin olive oil
2 eggplants, halved lengthways
4 tomatoes
5 0z. ball mozzarella, drained
1 handful of basil leaves
Salt and pepper, to taste
1 pinch sunflower seeds

Directions:
- Drizzle the oil over the eggplant and bake in the preheated oven (to 200C/fan 180C) for 25 minutes until softened.
- Meanwhile, slice the tomatoes and mozzarella, then arrange on top of the eggplant.
- Return to oven for another 5 mins or until the cheese has melted.
- Scatter over some basil leaves.

Serve with couscous and green salad with the sunflower seeds.

Eggplant Pasta

Preparation time: 40 minutes

Ingredients for 4 portions:
1 pound large eggplant,
1 tbsp. extra virgin olive oil
¼ tsp. garlic, minced
¼ tsp. red pepper flakes
1 small tomato, seeded and chopped
3 tbsp. heavy cream
1 tbsp. basil, chiffonade
2 tbsp. parmesan cheese, grated
1 tbsp. breadcrumbs
¼ cup pomegranate seeds
Kosher salt

Directions:
Peel the eggplant, leaving 1-inch of skin at the top and bottom. Slice the eggplant lengthwise into ¼-inch-thick slices. (I would use a mandolin for this.) Place the eggplant slices on a cooling rack set over the sink and generously sprinkle with kosher salt. Wait 15 minutes, flip, sprinkle again and wait another 15 minutes. Rinse thoroughly under cool water and gently squeeze out excess water. Place on paper towels and pat dry, then cut the slices into ¼-inch-wide strips so that they resemble linguine. Heat a 10-inch sauté pan over medium-high heat and add the oil. When it shimmers, add the garlic and red pepper flakes and toss for 10 seconds. Add the

eggplant and toss to coat. Add the tomato and toss for 15 to 20 seconds. Add the cream and toss for another 10 seconds. Finish with the basil and parmesan.

Transfer to a serving dish, top with breadcrumbs. Sprinkle the pomegranate seeds, toss and serve immediately.

Stuffed Zucchini

Preparation time: 30 minutes

Ingredients for 4 portions:

2 zucchini cut in length and cored (boat-shaped)
5 canned, pitted black olives, sliced
3 Oz. of feta cheese for the filling
5 Oz. of finely chopped parmesan or any cheese to liking for seasoning
½ of a medium-size onion, chopped
Zucchini kernel
3 tbsp. of extra virgin olive oil
3 tbsp. of chopped celeriac
7 Oz. cherry tomatoes
Salt, pepper and garlic to liking
1 pinch of dill weed or any herb to liking

Directions:

- Oil and season empty zucchini boats with salt and pepper.
- Stuff zucchini boats in layers with chopped celeriac, feta cheese, chopped onion.
- Add sliced black olives on top.
- Add upper layer with parmesan cheese.
- Pour some extra virgin olive oil and add some salt, pepper and herbs if you like.
- Bake the stuffed zucchini for 10 minutes in a preheated to 350°F/180°C oven.

Serve with fresh Cherry tomatoes.

Baked Vegetables with Béchamel Sauce

Preparation time: 30 minutes

Ingredients for 4 portions:
1 cup salsify, preferably canned
1 cup brussels sprouts
3 carrots, chopped
1 medium potato, cut coarsely
Broccoli or cauliflower, etc., to taste

Béchamel sauce:
2 tbsp. butter
2 tbsp. whole wheat flour
1 cup milk
1 tsp. nutmeg, grated
Salt, pepper, to taste

On top:
½ cup cheddar cheese, grated

Directions:
- Steam all the vegetables and set aside. You might need to cook them separately as the cooking time for every vegetable varies. I zap them in the microwave for a few minutes.

- Melt butter in a saucepan. Add the flour and mix it well. Cook on low heat for about 4-5 minutes, without allowing the flour to turn brown. I take my pan off the burner a few times when doing this in order to avoid browning of the flour.

- Stirring constantly, slowly add the milk in a thin stream and in small batches. (Here's what I do to avoid lumps in my white sauce - transfer the flour from the pan into a mug and add a little milk and mix it thoroughly. Then transfer it back to the pan and add the rest of the milk. The result? Completely lump-free sauce).

- Keep stirring and bring to a boil. Reduce the heat, add all the salt, pepper powder and the mustard paste.
- Finally add the cheese slices and mix well till the cheese melts. Simmer for a few more minutes till the sauce thickens.

- Arrange the vegetables in a baking dish, I use my 9" pie dish. Pour the sauce over it, sprinkle the grated cheese over it and bake in the oven (pre-heat the oven first) at 200 degrees C till the cheese starts to brown.

Serve with some brown whole wheat bread.

Low-Carb Mushroom Cauliflower Risotto

Preparation time: 30 minutes

Ingredients for 4 portions:
6 medium portobello mushrooms
1 cup vegetable broth
2 cups cauliflower, riced
¼ cup heavy cream
½ cup parmesan cheese
1 tbsp. extra virgin olive oil
2 cloves garlic
Salt and pepper to taste

Directions:
- In a food processor, process the cauliflower florets until they become the size of rice.
- In a pan or small pot, cook garlic and mushrooms in a tablespoon of extra virgin olive oil.
- When the garlic is fragrant, add vegetable broth and your riced cauliflower.
- Stir well over the low heat so that the whole dish simmers and cover. Let steam for 10 minutes.
- After it is cooked, let half of the vegetable broth evaporate in an opened pan and cook the cauliflower about 5-10 minutes more. When stirred, add the heavy cream, parmesan cheese and spices to your cauliflower rice.

Stir until parmesan has melted and serve.

Baked Spicy Potatoes

Preparation time: 10 minutes

Ingredients for 4 Servings:
2 ½ pounds potatoes (or 3 pounds for less spicy potatoes)
2 tbsp. olive oil
2 garlic cloves, minced (or maybe 1/2 tsp. garlic powder)
2 tsp. parsley, dried
1/2 tsp. cayenne
1/2 tsp. paprika
3/4 tsp. salt
1/2 tsp. pepper

Directions:
Preheat the oven to 450°F or 230°C. Pour the olive oil onto a
rimmed cookie sheet. Add the spices and mix with the olive oil.
Clean the potatoes and slice them into even wedges. Put the
potatoes on the cookie sheet and use your hands to coat the
potatoes with the olive oil mix. The baking time will vary depending
on how big your wedges are. I usually bake mine for 20 minutes,
take them out of the oven to flip them, and bake for another 10 – 15
minutes. If you want them crispier, just bake them for a few minutes
longer.

Baked Sweet Potatoes

Preparation time: 5 minutes

Ingredients for 4 Servings:
4 medium sweet potatoes, scrubbed

Directions:
Preheat the oven to 425°F or 220°C. Scrub sweet potatoes and pierce in several places with a sharp knife. Line a baking sheet with foil and place the potatoes on top. Bake for 45 minutes to an hour, depending on the size of the potatoes, until thoroughly soft and beginning to ooze. Remove from the heat.

Place on a plate or in a dish and allow to cool. Cover with plastic wrap and refrigerate (they will continue to ooze and sweeten). Serve cold (cut and remove the skin) or room temperature, or reheat for 20 to 30 minutes in a 350°F or 175°C oven.

Fried Vegetables

Preparation time: 15 minutes
Ingredients for 4 Servings:
1 tbsp. olive oil
1 medium onion, sliced thin
1 cup carrots, diagonally sliced
2 cups broccoli florets
2 cups sugar snap peas
1 large red bell pepper, cut into strips
1 tbsp. reduced sodium soy sauce
1 tsp. garlic powder
1 tsp. ginger, ground
2 tsp. sesame seed, toasted
salt and pepper, to taste

Directions:
- Heat the oil in wok or large deep skillet on medium-high heat.
- Add onion and carrots; stir fry 2 minutes.
- Add remaining vegetables; stir fry 5 to 7 minutes or until vegetables are tender-crisp.
- Add soy sauce, garlic powder and ginger; stir-fry until well blended.
- Sprinkle with sesame seed. Serve over cooked rice, if desired.

Curried Couscous with Vegetables

Preparation time: 15 minutes

Ingredients for 4 Servings:

1 large onion, cut in thin wedges

2 cups yellow summer squash and/or zucchini (2 medium), coarsely chopped

2½ oz. can tomatoes with jalapeno peppers, diced

2 cups water

2 5.7 oz. packages curry-flavor couscous mix

1 cup almonds, chopped toasted slivered

1/2 cup raisins (optional)

cilantro sprigs (optional)

salt and pepper, to taste

Directions:

- In a 3½ or 4 quart slow cooker, combine onion, summer squash, undrained tomatoes, the water, and the seasoning packets from couscous mixes.
- Cover and cook on low-heat setting for 4 to 6 hours or on high-heat setting for 2 to 3 hours.
- Stir in couscous.
- Turn off cooker.
- Cover and let stand for 5 minutes.
- Fluff couscous mixture with a fork.

To serve, sprinkle each serving with almonds and raisins.

Grilled Vegetables

Preparation time: 10 minutes

Ingredients for 4 Servings:
1 lb. cremini mushrooms, cleaned
2 cups cauliflower, cut into small florets
2 cups cocktail tomatoes
12 cloves garlic, minced
2 tbsp. olive oil
salt and pepper to taste
1 tbsp. fresh parsley, chopped
1 tsp. fresh Italian parsley leaves, chopped
1 tsp. basil leaves, chopped fresh
1/2 tsp. fresh rosemary leaves, finely chopped

Directions:
Preheat oven to 400°F or 200°C. In a bowl add all the mushrooms and veggies. Drizzle with olive oil then add fresh Italian parsley leaves, fresh basil leaves, fresh rosemary leaves, salt, pepper and toss until well combined. Dump the veggies onto a baking sheet and place in the preheated oven. Roast for 20 to 30 minutes or until mushrooms are golden brown and cauliflower is fork tender.
Garnish with fresh parsley before serving.

Stewed Beans in Tomato Sauce

Preparation time: 10 minutes

Ingredients for 4 Servings:
1 lb. dried white beans, such as Great Northern or cannellini, picked over, rinsed, and drained
1 onion, 1 half finely chopped (1/2 cup)
1 carrot, cut crosswise into thirds
1 celery stalk, cut crosswise into thirds
1 dried bay leaf
1 can (28 oz.) whole plum tomatoes, with juice
2 tbsp. extra-virgin olive oil, plus more for drizzling
2 garlic cloves, minced
1/8 tsp. red-pepper flakes
1 sprig rosemary
coarse salt and pepper, freshly ground

Directions:
Soak beans in water overnight. Drain, and transfer to a large pot. Cover beans with 4 inches water. Add the intact half of the onion, the carrot, celery, and bay leaf. Bring to a boil. Reduce heat and simmer until beans are tender but not bursting, about 1 hour. Drain and remove onion, carrot, celery, and bay leaf; discard. Pulse tomatoes, with juice, in a food processor until coarsely chopped. Heat oil in a medium heavy-bottomed pot over medium heat. Add

chopped onion, the garlic, and red-pepper flakes. Cook, stirring occasionally, until onion and garlic are tender but not browned, about 3 minutes. Add tomatoes and rosemary. Bring to a boil. Add beans and simmer, stirring occasionally, until tomato sauce thickens, about 20 minutes. Season with salt and pepper. Serve warm and drizzle with oil just before serving.

Kimchi Fried Rice

Preparation time: 15 minutes

Ingredients for 4 Servings:

1 cup kimchi, cut into thumbnail size pieces

7 oz. pack enoki mushrooms, root removed (optional),

3 cups steamed white short/medium grain rice – if it is freshly cooked, leave it out for 5 to 10 mins at room temperature to cool down before cooking.

1/2 tsp. garlic, minced

1/4 cup kimchi juice (liquid from the bottom of the kimchi container)

1/2 tbsp. sesame oil

1/2 tbsp. cooking oil

1 to 2 tbsp. roasted sesame seeds, to garnish

(optional) 1/2 stalk green onion, thinly sliced

(optional) seaweed, roasted, seasoned, shredded

Directions:

On medium high heat preheat a pan/wok and once heated, add the cooking oil and spread it well with a spatula. Add the garlic, stir it fast for about 10 seconds. Add the kimchi and stir until 80% of it is cooked. Optionally, add the mushrooms and mix them well for a few seconds. Reduce the heat to medium-medium low. Add the rice and the kimchi juice. Mix everything together thoroughly. Add the sesame oil and mix well. Remove from heat. Garnish with sesame seeds, green onion and seaweed strips.

Biryani Rice

Preparation time: 25 minutes
Ingredients for 4 Servings:
2 cups basmati rice
3 cloves garlic crushed in a garlic press
1 tsp. ground cumin
1/2 tsp. ground turmeric
1/4 tsp. cayenne pepper or to taste
salt and freshly ground black pepper
3 tbsp. olive or canola oil
4 tsp. lemon juice
1/4 cup fresh cilantro or parsley, chopped
4 cardamom pods
2⅔ cups veggie stock
Directions:
Wash the rice in several changes of water and drain. Cover
generously with fresh water and leave to soak for 30 minutes. Drain.
Pour the oil into a heavy, medium pan and set over medium-high
heat. Put the cardamom pods in the pan and sauté for about 10-15
seconds. Add garlic and sauté for another 10 seconds. Add veggie
stock, bring to a boil. Add lemon juice, cumin, turmeric, cayenne,
black pepper and salt. Add the drained rice and bring to a boil
again. Cover tightly, turn heat to very, very low, and cook for about
25 minutes or until rice is soft.

Vegan Paella

Preparation time: 20 minutes

Ingredients for 4 Servings:
2½ cups vegetable stock
1/2 tsp. saffron threads
1½ tbsp. olive oil
1 large red onion, sliced
1 yellow bell pepper, sliced
1 red bell pepper, sliced
1 cup brown mushrooms, sliced
3 cloves garlic, minced
1 cup bomba rice
2 roma tomatoes, chopped
1½ tsp. paprika, smoked
salt and pepper, freshly ground, to taste
1 cup green peas
1 can artichoke hearts, drained and chopped
1/2 cup parsley, chopped

Directions:
- Combine the stock and saffron threads in a medium saucepan and bring to the boil over high heat.
- Reduce heat to low and maintain a simmer.

- Meanwhile, heat paella pan on the stove with 1 - 1/2 tablespoons olive oil.
- Add onion to paella pan and sauté for 2 minutes.
- Add sliced red and yellow pepper and continue to sauté till softened, about 5 minutes.
- Add the mushrooms and garlic and sauté for 5 minutes or until it has softened slightly.
- Season liberally with salt and pepper. Increase heat to medium-high.
- Add bomba rice, tomato and smoked paprika and cook, stirring, for 1 minute until well mixed through.
- Reduce heat to medium-low.
- Add one-third of the saffron infused stock and stir until just combined.
- Let simmer uncovered for 5 minutes or until liquid is almost absorbed.
- Add the next third of the stock and cook for 5 minutes uncovered or until almost absorbed.
- Add remaining third of stock and cook for 5-10 minutes uncovered.
- Sprinkle surface of paella with peas and artichoke hearts.
- Cover entire pan in tin foil and leave to cook on a low heat for 12 minutes.
- After 12 minutes, turn heat off but leave the paella pan covered with tin foil for another 10 minutes.
- Remove tin foil after 10 minutes and garnish with parsley.

Rice with Fresh Vegetables

Preparation time: 20 minutes

Ingredients for 4 Servings:

2 tbsp. butter

1/2 cup orzo pasta or broken spaghetti

1 tbsp. extra-virgin olive oil

1 bunch asparagus, trimmed and chopped 1 carrot, cut into short matchsticks

2 shallots, chopped

2 cloves garlic, chopped

salt and pepper, freshly ground

2½ cups vegetable stock

1 cup long-grain white rice

1 tbsp. lemon zest, plus the juice of 1/2 lemon

1 tbsp. fresh thyme, chopped

1 bunch arugula, chopped

about 1 cup Parmigiano-Reggiano, grated

Directions: Melt the butter in a medium pot over medium-high heat. Add the pasta and cook until nutty and deep golden brown. Add the extra-virgin olive oil, 1 turn of the pan, then add the asparagus, carrot, shallots, garlic, salt and pepper. Cover and cook to sweat the vegetables, stirring occasionally, for 5 minutes. Stir in the stock, rice, lemon zest, thyme and browned pasta and bring to a boil. Cover the pot, lower the heat and simmer until the rice is just tender. Fold in the arugula, then stir in the lemon juice and cheese.

Eggplant Pasta

Preparation time: 15 minutes

Ingredients for 4 Servings:
1 pound large eggplant
1 tbsp. olive oil
1/4 tsp. garlic, minced
1/4 tsp. red pepper flakes
1 small tomato, seeded and chopped
3 tbsp. heavy cream
1 tbsp. basil, chiffonade
2 tbsp. parmesan cheese, grated
1 tbsp. breadcrumbs
1/4 cup pomegranate seeds
kosher salt

Directions:
Peel the eggplant, leaving 1 inch of skin at the top and bottom. Slice the eggplant lengthwise into 1/4-inch-thick slices. Place the eggplant slices on a cooling rack set over the sink and generously sprinkle with kosher salt. Wait 15 minutes, flip, sprinkle again, and wait another 15 minutes. Rinse thoroughly under cool water and gently squeeze out excess water. Place on paper towels and pat dry, then cut the slices into 1/4-inch-wide strips so that they resemble linguine. Heat a 10-inch sauté pan over medium-high heat and add

the oil. When it shimmers, add the garlic and red pepper flakes and toss for 10 seconds. Add the eggplant and toss to coat. Add the tomato and toss for 15 to 20 seconds. Add the cream and toss for another 10 seconds. Finish with the basil and parmesan. Transfer to a serving dish, top with breadcrumbs. Sprinkle the pomegranate seeds, toss and serve immediately.

Stuffed Mushrooms

Preparation time: 30 minutes

Ingredients for 4 Servings:
8 small/medium size Portobello mushrooms
1 small stalk celery
2 cloves garlic, finely chopped
1/2 slice ginger, fresh
1 large onion, finely chopped
2 small red bell peppers, finely chopped
3 tbsp. pine nuts
4 tbsp. olive oil
2 tsp. soy sauce
salt and pepper and/or chili, to taste

Directions:
Cut and finely dice the stems of the mushrooms. Precook mushroom stems, ginger, garlic and pepper in the olive oil. Stir in all other ingredients into the vegetable mix after it is removed from heat. Oil the mushrooms and put them on the baking pan. Stuff the mushrooms, mounding them with the mix generously. Cook in an oven for 15-20 minutes until the top forms a crispy crust. Top the cooked mushrooms with some fresh herbs for a nice decor.

Fried Tomatoes

Preparation time: 25 minutes

Ingredients for 4 Servings:
8 ripe plum tomatoes, halved
2 tbsp. basil leaves, fresh chopped
1 tbsp. oregano, dry
1 tbsp. basil, dry
2 tbsp. rosemary, sprigs
2 cloves garlic, minced
3 tbsp. olive oil
salt and pepper, to taste

Directions:
Add some olive oil onto the frying pan, placing tomatoes cut-sides up. Sprinkle them with all herbs and garlic and drizzle with olive oil on top. Cover and cook on a lower heat at least for 5 minutes, then remove the cover and have them cooked until browned underneath. Top with some fresh greenery and serve immediately.

Pasta

Farfalle with Pesto and Tomatoes

Preparation time: 30 minutes

Ingredients for 4 Servings:
1 lb. farfalle
2 cups cherry or regular tomatoes, halved or chopped into small pieces
6 oz. arugula (rucola)
1 clove garlic
1/4 cup fresh parsley leaves, chopped
1/4 cup cheese, grated
1/3 cup olive oil
salt and pepper, to taste

Directions:
Prepare all ingredients as the water boils and pasta is cooked. For pesto, mix arugula, parsley, walnuts and garlic in a blender until finely chopped. Add some cheese, salt and pepper, and some olive oil until the sauce is smooth. Put the pasta into the pan full of boiling of water, about 1/4 of a pan. Stir gently until pasta is cooked and drain it well. Place the pasta mixed with the pesto into the serving bowl. Toss well again. Add tomatoes and toss again.

Tip: Use the pasta cooking water if you wish to thin the sauce.

Fusille with Cashews, Goat Cheese and Dried Tomatoes

Preparation time: 30 minutes

Ingredients for 4 Servings:
8 oz. Fusille pasta
1 cup of dried Tomatoes, chopped
4 oz. goat cheese, soft, fresh, cut into cubes
1 tbsp. thyme, fresh
4 cloves of garlic, minced
1 tbsp. olive oil
1/2 cup cashew nuts
salt and pepper and other herbs, to taste

Directions:
Cook pasta in a pan 3/4 full of boiling water until done, then drain it.
Prepare all ingredients as the water boils and pasta is cooked. Add all ingredients: tomatoes, cheese, cashews.
Stir garlic, salt, pepper and olive oil. Serve with fresh leaves of thyme or basil.

Farfalle with Rocket, Olives and Goat Cheese

Preparation time: 20 minutes

Ingredients for 4 Servings:
7 oz. Farfalle pasta
1/4 cup of olives of different colors
4 oz. goat cheese, soft fresh, crushed by large pieces
8 oz. rocket bunch, torn by hand
1 tbsp. olive oil
salt and pepper, to taste

Directions:
- Cook pasta in a cooking pan 3/4 full of boiling water until done, then drain.
- Prepare all ingredients as the water boils and pasta is cooked.
- Put the cooked pasta into the serving bowl with olives, pieces of cheese, and rocket.
- Add some salt and pepper if needed and add the olive oil.

Classic Spaghetti with Mushrooms

Preparation time: 30 minutes

Ingredients for 4 Servings:
7 oz. spaghetti
2/3 pound Portobello or white mushrooms, sliced
1small onion or shallots
3 tbsp. flat-leaf parsley, chopped
3 cloves of garlic, minced
2 tbsp. cream
salt and pepper, to taste
1/2 cup of olive oil

Directions:
Cook pasta in a cooking pan 3/4 full of boiling water until done, then drain. Prepare all ingredients as the water boils and pasta is cooked. Heat the olive oil in a frying pan. Add garlic until it softens becomes fragrant. Add mushrooms with some salt and wait until they begin to brown. Stir in the cream and parsley and simmer gently at the lower heat. Toss mushrooms, mix with pasta in a serving bowl.

Tip: Add some slices of cheese and try adding 1/2 cup of the pasta cooking water instead of Cream.

Pasta a la Norma

Preparation time: 30 minutes

Ingredients for 4 Servings:
7 oz. bucatini or spaghetti
2 medium eggplants, sliced
1 small onion, minced
2/3 cup canned tomatoes, crushed, peeled
2 tbsp. ricotta cheese, grated
1 pinch basil leaves, fresh and torn by hand, to liking
5 cloves of garlic, minced
5 tbsp. olive oil
1tbsp. red chile flakes, crushed
salt and pepper, to taste

Directions:
Cook pasta in a cooking pan 3/4 full of boiling water until done, then drain. Prepare all ingredients as the water boils and pasta is cooked. Oil the sliced eggplant with olive oil and stir it in the baking sheet, adding salt to taste. Heat the olive oil in a frying pan. Add garlic until it softens becomes fragrant. Add the crushed tomatoes and bring to a boil seasoning with salt and pepper. When the sauce is ready, add pasta and eggplants and toss it with the sauce gently. Add the chopped basil leaves. Serve with ricotta on top.

Tip: Add some red pepper flakes to your liking.

Pizza:

Pizza Base Dough:

1. No Yeast Whole Wheat Dough:

Both types of pizza base can be baked before topping it with the ingredients.
If baked together with the toppings, it takes about 20 minutes for baking.
Preparation time: 45 minutes

Ingredients for 1 pizza (2-3 portions):
2 ½ cup whole-wheat flour, rye flour to liking
2 ¾ baking soda/powder
1 tbsp. extra virgin olive oil
1 tsp. salt
¾ to 1 cup water

Directions:
- Mix all dry ingredients.
- Add oil and ¾ cups of water.
- Stir until the dough forms a soft and not sticky ball. Knead on a floured surface for 3-4 minutes.
- Roll and toss out, then top with the desired ingredients.
- Baking time is up to 10 minutes (at 400 degrees).

The whole wheat dough is generally cooked faster than the regular.

2. Classic Homemade Dough recipe:
Preparation time: 1 hour 15 minutes

Ingredients for 1 pizza (2-3 portions):
1 and ¼ tsp. active dry yeast
2 and ¼ cup whole-wheat flour mixed with rye and oat flour
1 tsp. sugar, granulated
½ tsp. salt
2 tbsp. extra virgin olive oil
1 cup water
1 tsp. garlic powder (optional)

Directions:
- Mix the yeast, sugar and warm water in a bowl. 5 minutes later the yeast mixture must look creamy on top.
- Stir the yeast mixture and add to the bowl with whole-wheat flour, salt and extra virgin olive oil.
- Stand mixer will do the work for you. Turn the mixer on low speed and mix for 20 minutes until it comes together.
- Form the ball and coat it with extra virgin olive oil. Cover the ball with a cooking-towel and place the dough in a warm place and wait until it is doubled-sized.
- Roll the dough into a flat circle. Brush the top with the extra virgin olive oil and garlic powder to liking.

Tip: Homemade whole wheat dough can be cooked frozen up to 3 months. To freeze, portion the dough into balls, coat them with Olive oil and place them in freeze-bags into the refrigerator. Before you are ready to cook the pizza, wait 30 minutes after you take it from the refrigerator.

Margarita Pizza

Preparation time: 35 minutes

Ingredients for 1 pizza (2-3 portions):
Whole wheat pizza dough
1 roma tomato, thinly sliced
1 handful of fresh basil, chopped
7 Oz. mozzarella cheese, grated
Red pepper flakes, optional
For Homemade sauce:
1 tbsp. olive oil
1 small white onion, minced
3-4 cloves garlic, minced
1 cup crushed tomatoes
2 tbsp. tomato paste
2 tsp. sugar
½ tsp. dried basil
½ tsp. dried oregano
½ tsp. dried thyme
Salt and pepper, to taste

Directions: *For the sauce,* heat the oil in a small saucepan. Add onion and garlic and sauté for 4-5 minutes. Stir in the remaining ingredients and bring to a simmer. Meanwhile, brush the pizza base rolled in circle or any other shape with extra virgin olive oil. Top it with tomato sauce, roma tomatoes, and mozzarella.
Bake for about 10 minutes more. The pizza is done when the edges are crisp and light-brown. Remove from oven, top with basil and red pepper flakes and serve immediately hot.

Pizza with Pesto, Rucola and Dried Tomatoes

Preparation time: 45 minutes

Ingredients for 1 pizza (2-3 portions):
11 Oz. whole wheat pizza dough base, rolled thin
3 cup fresh rucola leaves
½ cup pesto
1/3 cup dried tomatoes
1 black pepper, freshly ground
½ cup extra virgin olive oil
½ cup mozzarella cheese, grated, for topping
Salt and pepper, to taste

Directions:
- Cover the baking tray with the paper to prevent from sticking.
- Place pizza base on it.
- Sprinkle bottom of dough with extra virgin olive oil and bake crust in a preheated to 350°F/180°C oven for several minutes.
- Remove from heat and set aside.
- Apply pesto on whole wheat pizza crust.
- Sprinkle with dried tomatoes and crumble the mozzarella cheese grated and pepper on top.
- Bake in an oven for 10 minutes more until the crust is light brown.
Remove from heat and top it with some rucola leaves.

Pizza with Mushrooms and Corn

Preparation time: 45 minutes

Ingredients for 1 pizza (2-3 portions):
11 Oz. whole wheat pizza base, rolled thin
½ cup parmesan cheese, minced
2-3 tbsp. mozzarella cheese, spread
2 cup pizza tomato sauce
1 onion, sliced
1 cup canned sweet corn
5-6 Portobello or white mushrooms, boiled and sliced
1 large tomato, sliced
3 tbsp. extra virgin olive oil
Oregano and other herbs, dry
Salt and pepper, to taste

Directions:
- Cover the baking tray with the paper to prevent from sticking.
- Place pizza base on it.
- Spread the pizza tomato sauce on the pizza base.
- Spread the mozzarella cheese all over the crust.
- Add parmesan generously.
- Place mushrooms, oregano, onion and corn on the pizza base.
- Top it with some cheese and oregano again.
- Drizzle some extra virgin olive oil.
- Bake for 10-15 minutes in an oven until the base becomes gold brown. Serve warm.

Pizza with Zucchini and Spinach

Preparation time: 45 minutes

Ingredients for 1 pizza (2-3 portions):

11 Oz. whole wheat pizza base, rolled thin
1 cup tomato pizza sauce
1 medium size zucchini, sliced
1 red bell pepper, finely chopped
1 cup raw spinach, chopped
1 onion, finely chopped
1 cup curd cheese, grated
1 cup mozzarella cheese, grated
3 cups extra virgin olive oil
Salt and pepper, to taste

Directions:
- Cover the baking tray with the paper to prevent from sticking.
- Apply tomato sauce generously and add some curd cheese, onion, pepper, spinach, zucchini and tomatoes onto the pizza base.
- Add some mozzarella cheese on top.
- Place pizza into the oven and bake it until it is golden brown.
- Remove from oven and serve warm.

Pizza with Olives, Pepper and Mushrooms

Preparation time: 45 minutes

Ingredients for 1 pizza (2-3 portions):
11 Oz. whole wheat pizza base, rolled thin
½ cup tomato pizza sauce
1 cup gorgonzola cheese, grated
½ cup of black olives, sliced
1 green bell pepper, cut into strips
1 onion, finely chopped
2 cloves garlic, minced
¼ tsp. dried oregano and other herbs
3 tbsp. extra virgin olive oil
Salt and pepper, to taste

Directions:
- Cover the baking tray with the paper to prevent from sticking.
- Place rolled in a circle or any other form pizza base on it.
- Spread tomato pizza sauce onto the base and sprinkle some herbs over it.
- Sprinkle some salt and extra virgin olive oil over the mushrooms and put them on the grill for a couple of minutes.
- Apply Gorgonzola cheese or other cheese to your liking, mushrooms, peppers, olives and green pepper on top.
- Add some more oregano and put the pizza into the oven, 15 minutes later remove and serve hot.

Cauliflower Pizza Crust with Cheese and Broccoli

Preparation time: 45 minutes

Ingredients for 1 pizza (2-3 portions):

For the crust:
1 small cauliflower head
2 eggs
½ cup parmesan cheese, grated
½ cup cheddar cheese
Oregano and other herbs
1 pinch garlic powder
Salt

For the topping:
½ cup tomato pizza sauce
1 bell pepper, striped
4 lb. broccoli, cut into pieces
1 small onion, striped
½ cup mozzarella cheese, crushed
4 portobello mushrooms, sliced
¼ tsp. dried oregano and other herbs
3 tbsp. extra virgin olive oil
Salt and pepper, to taste

Directions:

- Blend the cauliflower pieces in the food-processor until mixed.
- Place the cauliflower mass into a small pan with the boiling water for a 5 minutes steaming.
- When ready and cooled, use the cheese cloth for squeezing the extra water and thus prepare the cauliflower mass.
- Put it into the cooking bowl and mix with eggs, parmesan and cheddar cheese.
- Oil the baking tray or the baking paper well and spread the mass evenly on it.
- Sprinkle oregano and other herbs or seeds, some garlic powder and salt atop.
- Put it into the preheated oven for 10 minutes at 350grades.
- Remove from the oven and spread the cauliflower crust with the tomato pizza sauce.
- Place the vegetable ingredients randomly over the top and again place the pizza into the oven for 15 minutes at the same temperature.

Tip: Broccoli can be used the same method for the crust instead of cauliflower.

Spinach Pizza Crust

Preparation time: 45 minutes

Ingredients for 1 pizza (2-3 portions):

For the crust:
6 Oz. fresh spinach, crushed
2 eggs
1 cup any Italian cheese, shredded
Salt and pepper
Seeds to liking

For the topping:
½ cup tomato pizza sauce
5 cherry tomatoes, cut into pieces
1 small onion, finely chopped
4 portobello mushrooms, sliced
¼ tsp. dried oregano and other herbs
3 tbsp. extra virgin olive oil
Salt and pepper, to taste

Directions:
- Heat the oven to +400 grades beforehand.
- Prepare the baking parchment paper as it is the right way to keep the crust whole.
- Blend the spinach until it is the paste consistency.
- Add eggs, cheese and spices and pulse until combined.
- Spread the mixture onto the paper in the pizza pan. Bake it about 15 minutes until edges are browned at 350 or 400 grades.

- Spread the tomato pizza sauce over the top of the crust and place the toppings.
- Place back into the oven and cook until the mushrooms get softer and cheese melts, not more than 15 minutes more.

Tip: Spinach is a good choice for individuals with allergies and is equally delicious when cold

Sandwiches

Hot Sandwich with Mushrooms and Cheese

Preparation time: 15 minutes

Ingredients for 4 Servings:
4 slices of any bread to your liking
5 Portobello mushrooms
1 medium onion, sliced
2 cloves garlic
1 lb. cheese
1 tomato, sliced
thyme, dry
2 tbsp. Dijon, to taste
salt and pepper, to taste

Directions:
Sautee mushrooms with onion and garlic, salt and pepper, and thyme. Apply 4 slices of bread with cheese and add some mushroom mixture and Dijon mustard on top. Cover with the remaining 4 slices of bread. Put into the preheated oven for 5 minutes. Serve hot.

Hot Sandwich with Zucchini and Tomatoes

Preparation time: 15 minutes

Ingredients for 4 Servings:
4 ciabatta rolls, split, toasted
1 zucchini, cut lengthwise into 6 slices
1 tomato, sliced
mozzarella cheese, thinly sliced
8 large basil leaves, fresh
1½ tbsp. balsamic vinegar
4 tsp. of olive oil
1/8 tsp. black pepper, freshly ground
salt, to taste

Directions:
Toss zucchini in the cooking bowl with garlic and 2 teaspoons of olive oil. Place zucchini into the grill oven for 2-5 minutes. Remove from grill and sprinkle with vinegar, salt and pepper.
Sprinkle the roll slices with olive oil and put the basil leaves, mozzarella cheese, slices of zucchini, tomato, and onion and cover them with the remaining halves of the rolls. Heat the sandwiches in an oven and serve hot.

Hot Sandwich with Spinach and Mushrooms

Preparation time: 20 minutes

Ingredients for 4 Servings:
4 slices of toast bread/plain bread/4 rolls, split in half
10 oz. Portobello mushrooms, cleaned and sliced
2 pinches of fresh spinach, torn or cut
1 bell pepper, sliced
1/2 cup pickled onion
1 clove garlic, minced
1 cup cheddar cheese, shredded
cilantro, to taste
1tbsp. olive oil
salt and pepper, freshly ground
1/4 cup water

Directions:
Cook mushrooms in a frying pan, adding olive oil and bell pepper. Season with salt, pepper and garlic. Add spinach and onion and some water, gently tossing the mixture. Add cheddar cheese and remove from heat. Spread the mixture on 4 halves of rolls, add cilantro and remaining cheese on the top halves of the rolls. Close the roll and serve.

Tip: Put them into a preheated oven if you like them hot.

Sandwich with Fried Cheese and Salted Green Tomatoes

Preparation time: 15 minutes

Ingredients for 4 Servings:
4 rolls, split in half
butter
4 slices pimento grilled cheese
2 green tomatoes, large
1 handful herbs, fresh
1 red onion
5 tbsp. olive oil
salt and pepper, to taste

Directions:
Butter both sides of the bread. Put the slices of cheese into the grill oven for 2 minutes and then remove. Layer the rolls with grilled cheese, tomato slices, fresh herbs and onion. Close the rolls and put them into the grill or bake them for 5 minutes more if you want to serve them hot.

Sandwich with Rocket and Goat Cheese

Preparation time: 10 minutes

Ingredients for 4 Servings:
8 slices of granary bread
butter
2 oz. rocket, fresh
1/2 red onion, finely sliced
1/2 cup sun-dried tomatoes
3 oz. goat cheese, soft finely cut
2 tbsp. olive oil

Directions:
Spread butter over 4 pieces of bread. Layer the goat cheese on top of each. Add seasoning salt, slices of onion, dried tomatoes and rucola leaves generously. Sprinkle some olive oil on top. Serve cold.

Keto Breads:

Garlic Parmesan Focaccia

Preparation time: 45 minutes

Ingredients:
2 tbsp. basil, dry
2 tbsp. rosemary, dry
2 tbsp. thyme, dry
2 tbsp. rapid yeast
1 tbsp. salt
½ tbsp. pepper
¼ cup extra virgin olive oil and
1tbsp. extra virgin olive oil
1 cup water
4 cup whole wheat flour
½ cup parmesan cheese, grated
2 cloves garlic, minced

Directions:
Mix the yeast in a warm water, with some pinch of sugar(optionally). Set aside the mixture for 5 minutes, then place it into the mixer bowl with the flour, salt and ¼ cup of extra virgin olive oil. Have your dough kneaded and let it rise for 40 minutes in a warm place. Oil the baking tray and spread your dough onto the baking sheet. Drizzle some olive oil onto the focaccia and add the parmesan cheese with the minced garlic with all the herbs on top of your dough layer and place it into the preheated to 350°F/180°C oven. Bake for 20 minutes and enjoy warm.

Coconut Flour Pineapple Bread

Preparation time: 75 minutes

Ingredients:
20 Oz. canned pineapple pieces in juice
1 cup coconut, grated or shredded
½ cup whole wheat flour
1 cup water
½ cup butter
2 eggs
½ tsp. baking soda
½ tsp. salt
1 cup sour cream

Directions:
Preheat the oven. Allow pineapple to sit and drain for 10 minutes in a bowl. Spread coconut on a large rimmed baking sheet. Bake it, tossing occasionally up to 10 minutes. Oil the bottom and sides of a loaf pan and dust it with flour. In a separate bowl, mix the flour, baking soda, and salt. In a mixer, beat the butter on high speed until fluffy. Add eggs. Little by little, add the dry flour mixture and sour cream gradually. Mix all ingredients until combined. Fold pineapple into the dough and ½ cup toasted coconut. Place your dough mixture into the loaf pan and sprinkle with remaining ½ cup coconut. Bake for an hour. Let cool in pan 15 minutes. Remove from pan.

Tips: Adding any nuts to this bread would make it even more nutritious.

Banana Bread

Preparation time: 45 minutes

Ingredients:
3 bananas, 1 ½ cup mashed
2 cups all-purpose flour
1 cup water
½ cup butter, unsalted, melted
2 eggs
1 cup walnuts, chopped
½ cup brown sugar
1 tsp. cinnamon, ground
1 tsp. vanilla extract
1 tsp. baking soda
1 tsp. salt

Directions:
- Preheat the oven until it is about 200 degrees C.
- Grease the loaf pan with the butter and drizzle with some flour.
- Bake the nuts for 5 minutes, and combine when cooled with flour, baking soda, sugar, cinnamon and salt.
- In a bowl combine eggs, butter and bananas. Mix this mixture with the dry ingredients until the batter is thick, but soft. Scrape it into the loaf pan.

Bake it for about 60 -70 minutes and remove from oven when crusty.

Cheesy Herb Bread

Preparation time: 75 minutes

Ingredients:
12Oz. flour
1 cup water
1 pinch of sugar
½ cup butter, melted
2 eggs
Dry yeast
2 tbsp. basil, dry
2 tbsp. rosemary, dry
2 tbsp. thyme, dry
2 tbsp. rapid yeast
Any cheese, to taste
1 pinch salt

Directions:
- Mix flour, baking soda, salt, sugar in a bowl, then add the water, beaten eggs, butter.
- Mix the mass with the herbs and cheese and knead it adding some flour until a bit sticky.
- Set aside for 30 minutes covered with a napkin.
- Grease the loaf pan and place your dough into it dusting on top with the remaining herbs.
- Let it rest a couple of minutes and place into the preheated to 350°F/180°C oven.

Bake for 40 minutes until it turns light brown and ready.

Coconut Flour Bread

Preparation time: 45 minutes

Ingredients:
½ cup coconut flour
1/3 tapioca flour
1/3 cup linen flour (flax meal)
2tsp. baking powder
4 eggs
1 cup avocado oil
½ cup coconut milk
Sesame seeds
Coconut flakess
Directions:
• Keep your oven preheated to 350°F/180°C.
• Place the parchment paper for lining the loaf pan.
• You can mix all the ingredients in a blender until fully mixed.
• Fill the batter dough into the pan and sprinkle sesame seeds and
coconut flakes. Bake the bread for 30 minutes until a toothpick
inserted in the bread comes out clean.
Let it cool and store in the fridge or else it quite easily becomes dry.

Keto Breakfast Pockets with Curd Filling

Preparation time: 45 minutes

Ingredients:

For the filling:
½ mozzarella cheese
½ cup low-moisture curd
1 egg
1 tbsp. cream cheese
1 pinch salt

For the dough:
4 cups whole-wheat flour
½ Oz. package dry yeast
1 cup water, warm
3 cups milk
1 egg
½ cup Extra Virgin Olive oil
1 pinch sugar
1 tsp. salt
Linen or sesame seeds

Directions:

Mix the yeast with sugar in a warm water, add the milk, Olive oil, egg, 2 cups of flour and salt, mix until combined. Add the flour to form a sticky dough. Cover it with a napkin and let rise for at least 30 minutes in a warm place. Meanwhile prepare the filling, mixing the cheese, salt and egg. Divide the dough into 10-12 pieces. Roll each dough piece into circle and top them with the curd filling. Fold the dough over and pinch the edges to seal. Grease the baking tray and place the pockets onto the tray. Bake until light brown for about 20 minutes.

Almond Flour Crepes

Preparation time: 45 minutes

Ingredients:
1 cup almond flour
1 cup water
4 eggs
1 tbsp. extra virgin coconut oil
1 pinch cinnamon

Directions:
- Beat the eggs, whisk them with the cinnamon, almond flour until combined.
- You can use a crepe pan non-stick bottom or any pan for frying, on the medium heat.
- Pour the crepe mixture into the pan and tilt the pan round to cover the surface evenly. Cook it until edges become crispy each side for 3 minutes. Both sides should be light brown.
- Cook your crepes regulating the thickness of crepes by changing the scoop.
- To serve fill the crepes with a low carb sweet or salty and savoury filling.

Desserts:

Cheesecake

Preparation time: 45 minutes

Ingredients:

For the crust:

4 tbsp. butter

6 cups coconut, shredded

Any sweetener you consider appropriate

8 Oz. cream cheese

½ cup stevia sweetener

½ maple syrup

16 Oz. can of pineapple in a syrup, crashed or whole, drained

¼ cup whipping cream

5 eggs

Directions:

- After you mix all the crust ingredients press evenly and place it into the baking tray or pan and have it baked for at least 10 minutes. Let it cool.
- In a blender mix well the cream cheese with sweeteners, the pineapple until blended.
- Add the eggs gradually and pour this batter into the pan you have prepared.
- Bake for 90 minutes. Remove from oven and let it cooled.
  Tip: Can be served with additional pineapple on top and/or with whipped cream whatever topping you choose to your liking.

Gluten-Free Nutella Brownie Trifle

Preparation time: 60 minutes
Ingredients:
For the brownies:
6 Oz. hazelnuts
½ cup almonds
½ cup cashews
1 cup medjool dates, pitted
½ tsp. vanilla extract
2 tbsp. cacao powder
2 tbsp. hazelnut butter
1 tbsp. maple syrup or honey, to taste

For the frosting:
½ cup avocado, fresh crushed
1 ½ tbsp. coconut oil
½ tsp. vanilla
2tbsp. coconut maple syrup
1 tbsp. cacao
1 tbsp. nut butter

Directions:
- You will need some baking paper for lining the baking tray.
- Dry the hazelnuts and almonds in a frying pan until toasted.
- Add ¾ of all the nuts with the almonds into the food processor until they are broken to chunks.
- Add the dates and process again, then all the rest ingredients until you have a sticky mass.
- Pour it onto the baking tray lined with paper. Press the crumbly mixture you made with your fingers until the top of it is even. Place into the fridge while you are cooking the glaze.

- For the glaze you will have to mix well all the ingredients in a bowl or process them all in a food processor until well combined. It should be smooth and creamy.
- Remove your brownie from a fridge add the frosting on top spreading it evenly.
- Top the brownie with the remaining nuts and place again into the fridge until you have it served.

Low-Carb Curd Soufflé

Preparation time: 45 minutes

Ingredients:
For the soufflé:
7 Oz. cream
½ cup condensed milk
1 pack (1 Oz.) gelatin for a dense soufflé
1 cup milk
5 Oz. cottage cheese

Directions:
- Fill the gelatin with milk and set aside.
- Mix the condensed milk with the cream and bring to boil on a low heat.
- Pour the gelatin mass into the boiled mixture and mix it, then let it cool.
- In a mixer, have all the mass combined well with the cottage cheese for at least 10 minutes.
- Pour it into the silicone moulds for the cupcakes and let it freeze for a couple of hours and serve.

Cream Cheese Cookies

Preparation time: 40 minutes

Ingredients:
1 cup butter
¾ cup stevia or any sugar substitute
4 Oz. cream cheese, softened
1 egg
2 cups almond flour
1 cup coconut flour
Sesame seeds
Vanilla or any flavored extract to taste

Directions:
- Mix the butter with the sweetener until fluffy.
- Beat the cream cheese and add the egg, then flour and mix it with the flavor and seeds you have chosen.
- Let it chill for 3-4 hours.
- Roll the cookie mass into a log and have it sliced thus forming your cookies.

Bake until brown up to 15 minutes or more to make them crispy.

Chia Seeds Pudding with Berries

Preparation time: 60 minutes

Ingredients:
2 cups coconut milk, full fat
1 banana, sliced
½ cups chia seeds
Honey or stevia for sweetening
5 Oz. at least any fresh berries

Directions:
- Stir the milk, chia seeds and stevia (or honey) in a mixing bowl.
- Add half of all the berries and let the mixture chilled for at least 1 hour.
- Mix it up again and add the berries and banana before serving.

Tip: Chia seeds have omega-3 fatty acids, protein, fiber, calcium and antioxidants.

Smoothie Bowl

Preparation time: 45 minutes

Ingredients:
6 Oz. berries, fresh or frozen
2 medium frozen bananas
½ cup Almond milk
1 cup jellified yoghurt
1 tbsp. Chia seeds
1 tbsp. Hemp seeds
1 tbsp. Coconut flakes
Raspberry jam or any other, to taste

Directions:
- In a blender mix the bananas with half of the berries until it has a puree consistency.
- Organise your smoothie in a bowl decorating it in rows with the yogurt spot, the puree and fresh berries and with a pinch of seeds and flakes you have.

Coconut milk smoothie

Preparation time: 15 minutes

Ingredients:
1 cup Greek yogurt
1 cup coconut milk, full fat
1 banana, fresh or frozen
1 cup baby spinach, fresh
1 tbsp. honey
5 Oz. blueberries or other berries

Directions:
In a blender mix all the ingredients until smooth. Add the ice for a thicker smoothie.

Yogurt Smoothie with Cinnamon and Mango

Preparation time: 15 minutes

Ingredients:
4 Oz. frozen mango chunks, mango pulp or fresh mango
1 cup Greek yogurt
1 cup coconut milk, full fat
3-4 cups milk
3 tbsp. flax seed meal
1 tbsp. honey
1 tsp. cinnamon

Directions:
In a blender mix all the ingredients, except cinnamon until smooth.
Sprinkle each smoothie with a pinch of cinnamon.

Lemon Curd Dessert (Sugar Free)

Preparation time: 35 minutes

Ingredients:
½ cup unsalted butter
½ cup lemon juice
2 tbsp. lemon zest
6 egg yolks
Stevia for sweetening

Directions:
- On a low heat melt the butter in a saucepan.
- Whisk in the stevia or any other sweetener, lemon ingredients until combined, then add the egg yolks and return to the stove again over the low heat.
- Whisk it until the curd starts thickening.
- Strain into a small bowl and let cool.

Can be stored in a fridge for several weeks.

Chocolate Almond Butter Smoothie

Preparation time: 35 minutes

Ingredients:
2 tbsp. chocolate protein powder
½ tbsp. cacao powder
1 cup almond milk
2 tbsp. almond butter
1 fresh banana
½ cup fresh strawberries
1 tbsp. chia or hemp seeds
Maple syrup or stevia for sweetening

Directions:
Put all the ingredients into the blender and mix until it has creamy consistency.

Berry and Nuts Dessert

Preparation time: 25 minutes

Ingredients for 2 portions:
10 Oz. yogurt or yogurt drink
7 Oz. strawberries, fresh
Blueberries, raspberries or any berries you may like
1 banana, sliced
Pinch of Pistachio
Pinch of cashews
4 walnuts, shelled
Pinch of pumpkin seeds
Pinch of sunflower seeds
Several fresh mint leaves

Directions:
In a serving dish pour the jellied yogurt and top it with all the fresh ingredients.

Pastry with Nuts, Mango and Blueberries

Preparation time: 45 minutes

Ingredients:
For the pastry:
1 cup whole wheat flour
½ cup whole wheat almond flour
½ cup butter
2 eggs yolks
2 Oz. water
12 Oz. blueberries or any berries to your liking
2 Mangoes
1 pinch of pumpkin seeds
Sesame and sunflower seeds
Peanuts, dried

For the filling:
8 Oz. cream cheese
1 mango, chopped
½ icing sugar
2 tbsp. lemon juice

Directions:
- In a bowl mix the flour ingredients with the butter, add the egg yolks and some water until combined and forms a ball.
- Knead the dough a little until it is smooth and refrigerate for half an hour covered with a napkin.
- Mix all the ingredients of the pastry filling in a blender.
- Grease your baking tray or a cooking tin and dust with some flour.

- Pour the dough into the tin and bake for 30 minutes (200 grades) until lightly brown.
- Pour the filling onto the pastry and top it with berries and nuts. Add some dessert sauce for serving.

Keto Vegan Pumpkin Mousse

Preparation time: 15 minutes

Ingredients:
15 oz. firm Tofu
15 oz. organic Pumpkin
1 tbsp. Cinnamon
½ tsp. Ginger
Stevia for sweetening

Directions:
Mix all the ingredients in a blender until smooth. Taste and add
more stevia for sweetening.

Keto Flax Seed Waffles

Preparation time: 20 minutes

Ingredients for 4 portions:
2 cups Golden Flax Seed
1 tbsp. Baking Powder
5 tbsp. Flax Seed Meal (mixed with 15 tbsp. Water)
⅓ cup Avocado Oil
½ cup Water
1 tsp. Sea Salt
1 tbsp. fresh Herbs (thyme, rosemary or parsley) or 2 tsp. cinnamon, ground

Directions:
- Preheat the waffle-maker.
- Combine the flax seed with baking powder with a pinch of salt in a bowl. Whisk the mixture.
- Place the jelly-like flax seed mixture, some water and oil into the blender and pulse until foamy.
- Transfer the liquid mixture to the bowl with the flax seed mixture. Stir until combined. The mixture must be fluffy.
- Once it is combined, set aside for a couple of minutes. Add some fresh herbs or cinnamon. Divide the mixture into 4 servings.
- Scoop each, one at a time, onto the waffle maker. Cook with the closed top until it's ready. Repeat with the remaining batter.
- Eat immediately or keep in an air-tight container for a couple of weeks.

Keto Lemon Fat Bombs

Preparation time: 60 minutes

Ingredients (for approx. 30 fat bombs):
1 cup Coconut Oil, melted
2 cups Raw Cashews, boiled for 10 minutes, soaked
½ cup Coconut Butter
1 Lemon Zest
2 Lemons, juiced
¼ cup Coconut Flour
⅓ cup Coconut, shredded
A pinch of salt
Stevia for sweetening

Directions:
- Mix all the ingredients in a food processor and blend until combined.
- Place the mixture to a bowl and have it cooled up in the freezer to 40 minutes.
- Remove from freezer and make the balls.
- Place them onto the cooking tray and again place into the freezer for hardening.
- Remove from the freezer and store in an air-tight container for up to a week. Let them thaw before serving.

Candied Pecans

Preparation time: 60 minutes

Ingredients for 4 portions:
6 oz. Whole Pecans
½ cup Aquafaba
1 oz. Palm Sugar
1 oz. whole Green Cardamom Pods
¼ tsp. Salt
1 tsp. Allspice

Directions:
- Pre-heat oven to 350°F/180°C.
- Prepare a baking tray with a piece of parchment paper.
- Remove the cardamom seeds from the pods. Crush the seeds and lay them onto one side of the tray.
- Chop the sugar or grind it in a food processor.
- Whisk the aquafaba until frothy, stir in the sugar and salt. Fold in the nuts, allspice, cardamom, until everything is coated.
- Spread the mixture evenly over the baking tray for about 15 minutes and replace it onto the cooling rack.

When cooled, pecans can be enjoyed as a topping or as they are.

Made in the USA
Lexington, KY
10 November 2019